THE SOLDIER AND THE WOMAN

A Play in One Act

by

ELAINE MORGAN

SAMUEL FRENCH

FRENCH

LONDON

NEW YORK SYDNEY TORONTO HOLLYWOOD

ISBN 0 573 06234 X

Printed in Great Britain by W & J Mackay & Co Ltd, Chatham

HN71901

THE SOLDIER AND THE WOMAN

Produced on B.B.C. Television on the 29th December 1960, with the following cast of characters:

(in the order of their appearance)

SIMON, an innkeeper	*Colin Blakely*
RACHEL, his wife	*Rosalie Crutchley*
AN OFFICER	*Thomas Heathcote*
A SOLDIER	*Douglas Blackwell*

The action of the Play passes in the stable of an inn in Bethlehem

SCENE I

Early morning

SCENE II

Late afternoon

SCENE I

SCENE—*The stable of an inn in Bethlehem. Early morning.*

The only door is across the corner up R *and there is an unglazed window in the wall* R. *Up* L, *there are three stalls, with their doors facing* R, *so that the interiors are unseen. Down* L *there is a long, sturdy rough-hewn bench, about six feet long, three feet wide, and of a height convenient for milking or for resting a bucket on while mixing a mash for pigs. A bucket and an opened sack of grain stand on the bench. Between the bench and the stalls are some sacks of grain. On the wall down* L *there is a shelf for wine jars. Under the window* R *there is a manger, with hay in it. The hay is flattened and hollow. The manger has recently been repaired and three of the slats gleam new wood. A milking stool stands down* C. *There is a quantity of loose hay in the corner down* L *and scattered about the floor. Various wooden and earthenware implements of rural husbandry are in evidence.*

When the CURTAIN *rises, rural morning noises filter in through the open door—crowing and lowing and the rattle and splash of a well-bucket.* RACHEL *is unseen in one of the stalls. She is in her early twenties, strong and dark and full of life.* SIMON, *the innkeeper, appears at the door. He is aged about thirty-five and is stolid, anxious and preoccupied with his business cares.*

SIMON (*calling*) Rachel!

(RACHEL *emerges from the stall. She looks pleased with herself*)

RACHEL. Here.

(SIMON *grunts*)

SIMON. Oh. (*He comes into the stable, closes the door and looks around him in surprise*) Where are they?
RACHEL. They're gone.
SIMON. When?
RACHEL. In the night.
SIMON (*looking towards the manger*) What—with the baby and all?
RACHEL. Of *course*, with the baby.
SIMON. Oh. (*He sounds hurt and disillusioned*) I see.
RACHEL. What's the matter?
SIMON (*crossing to the bench down* L) Oh, nothing. (*He mixes a mess of husks in the bucket for the pigs*) Not the first time people have skipped

in the night—but I can usually tell that kind right away. I wouldn't have expected it of that pair, somehow.

(Rachel *smiles secretly to herself, but lets Simon go on*)

She wasn't barely fit to travel, was she?

Rachel (*crossing to the manger*) Oh, she was all right. She was a lot stronger yesterday.

Simon. Mm! So she should be. I saw Martha sneaking out of the kitchen five or six times a day taking her bits of the best of everything. (*Slightly bitter*) I suppose they were afraid I was going to charge them for that.

Rachel (*testing the gleaming new slats in the manger*) He made a good strong job of mending the manger.

Simon (*still disgruntled*) So he should, it's his trade. I suppose they reckon that'll count as payment in kind. Some'll do anything rather than part with cash. (*He crosses to the manger and examines it*) It was well enough as it was before. (*He is determined not to be mollified*) It was only meant for hay. Anybody'd think it had to hold the weight of the world.

Rachel (*crossing to c; softly*) I expect their baby is all the world to them, the same as ours is to us.

Simon (*still hurt; it is not the money that bothers him*) I wouldn't have minded if they'd come to me—if they were really hard up, I mean, if they'd come to me fair and square, the way they came that first night, and said straight out, "Look here, landlord, we're in a fix". But it shows you, doesn't it, what opinion they had of *me*, after I'd done my best for them—if they felt they had to go off in the middle of the night with her as weak as she was. What did they think I'd have done to them? (*He shakes his head*) No, it beats me.

(Rachel, *smiling almost mischievously, moves to* l *of Simon and holds out something to him in her hand.* Simon, *puzzled, extends his palm and* Rachel *puts two coins in it*)

(*Astonished*) It's gold!

(Rachel *nods*)

He gave you this?

(Rachel *nods, still smiling*)

When?

Rachel. Last night.

Simon. You were here when they went, then?

Rachel. Yes. I helped them to pack.

(Simon *examines the coins and bites one, vaguely uneasy and suspicious*)

Simon. How'd he get hold of this kind of money?

Rachel. Those foreigners brought it, remember? And *she* gave me this. (*She produces a pot of frankincense, removes the lid and holds it up to Simon*) Smell. That was a present, too.

Simon (*half to himself*) But *why?*

Rachel (*inclined to be resentful, as if she were thought unworthy*) You mean—why did she give it to me?

Simon (*thinking hard*) No, I mean why did *they* give it to *her?* I just couldn't see what they were making all the fuss about, it was only a baby.

Rachel (*deprecatingly*) Oh, well—fakirs, Simon. They always act a bit queer. Maybe they think new babies are lucky.

(Simon *is unconvinced and tosses the gold in his palm, wondering*)

Simon. All the same, I wish we could have understood what they were saying.

Rachel. I only wish they'd come a month ago when our David was born, then perhaps they'd have given the things to me. Because I'm sure this one couldn't have been a patch on David. I felt like bringing him out yesterday and telling them, "If you think *that* baby's worth making a fuss about, what about *this* one?" (*Her face and voice are radiant with the ineffable complacency of new motherhood*) But then I thought—(*tolerantly*) "No, David's a month older, it wouldn't be fair to compare them." What was He like? Theirs? It *was* a boy, wasn't it?

Simon. Mm? Boy—yes.

Rachel. What did they call Him?

Simon. I never heard.

Rachel. That was why I really came out here last night. It was the first proper chance I'd had, with the place so full. I thought, "It's coming to something, there's all this excitement about it, and it's *our* stable, after all, and me so rushed off my feet I must be nearly the only one that hasn't seen it."

Simon. *Did* you see Him?

Rachel. Not properly, even then. She had Him all wrapped up ready to go, and I didn't like to ask her to undo Him; it was so cold. (*She smiles*) I could see His little nose, that's all.

Simon (*curiously*) You didn't see His eyes?

Rachel. No, He was sleeping. Why? Was there anything wrong with His eyes?

Simon. Oh, no. Nothing *wrong*.

Rachel (*jealous at something in Simon's voice*) David's got beautiful eyes. (*Her own eyes flash indignantly*)

Simon (*amused and tender*) Yes, he has. Like his mother's.

Rachel (*appeased; almost purring over the richness of her life*) Mmmmm. Almost time for his feed. (*She stretches, feeling liberated*)

I'll have a bit more time to give to him today; it's nice to think the rush is over now till next time.

Simon (*collecting himself*) We must get a few rooms ready right away, though.

Rachel (*dismayed*) What for now?

Simon. There was a messenger from Jerusalem, an hour ago; they want some rooms prepared for their officers.

Rachel (*startled*) Officers? (*Her face closes with hatred*) Herod's men!

Simon (*stolidly*) Yes.

Rachel (*bitterly*) Do we have to put up Herod's men?

Simon. You know we do.

Rachel. How long will they be staying?

Simon. I don't know.

Rachel (*agitated*) What are they coming here for?

Simon (*shrugging*) He said he didn't know what it was about, but at the rate they were riding they'd be here long before noon. Herod's half out of his mind again about something, and he's got them all as jumpy as crickets.

Rachel. Couldn't you tell them we're full?

Simon. But we're not, now.

Rachel (*half beseeching*) You could say we were.

Simon. Why would I want to say that? Their money's as good as anybody else's.

Rachel (*bitterly*) Is it?

Simon. Of course it is. (*Defensively; blustering a little*) Oh, I know the things people say about Herod; but I dare say it's not all his fault; he's got to keep in with the Romans, hasn't he, or he'd be finished.

(Rachel *regards Simon coldly and without sympathy*)

(*He grows more heated*) Well, it's true, isn't it? I mean, you've got to speak as you find, that's what I say—and if you ask me, it was *time* we had a strong man running things.

(Rachel *is silent and scornful*)

(*He goes on, frowning and not looking at Rachel*) Look how much better the roads are. And not half the crime, either. At one time it wasn't hardly safe to travel, bandits and murderers everywhere.

Rachel. I can well believe Herod wouldn't put up with that. He'd rather do all the murdering himself.

Simon. Now, look—where's the point of talking like that? Has he ever done anything to *us*? No. Well, then. I don't say he's not— I don't say he's . . . (*His eyes dart unconsciously to the door. He sidesteps even this furtive criticism*) But anyway, it's none of our business. (*He mutters to himself, rattled*) If you're running an inn, you can't afford to have—ideas about things like that—pick and choose. Take people as they come. (*Brusquely*) Come on, they'll be here soon. (*He takes the frankincense from her*) We can sprinkle some of this in their bed-rooms.

RACHEL (*grabbing the pot from him; alarmed*) No!

SIMON. *Now* what's the matter?

RACHEL. I don't want them asking questions.

SIMON. What do you mean—"questions"?

RACHEL (*hiding the pot under the pile of hay* R) About those people. (*Agitated*) Put that money away.

(SIMON *looks blank*)

(*Impatiently*) Those people last night.

SIMON. You mean—the carpenter? What makes you think they'd want to . . . ? (*He dries up, struck with a fearful surmise*)

RACHEL (*with a transparent pretence of calm*) I don't suppose they will—why should they? There's nothing to show there's been *anybody* here, is there? (*She moves to the manger and tries to ruffle up the hay. It is not very convincing*) Come on, let's fill it up. (*She crosses to* L, *collects an armful of hay from one of the stalls then crosses towards the manger*)

SIMON (*intercepting Rachel*) Rachel. What have you been doing?

RACHEL. Nothing. (*She drops the hay and stands still*)

SIMON. Who were they?

RACHEL. I don't know who they were. Joseph somebody. You ought to know, you saw more of them than I did.

SIMON. Why did they leave in the middle of the night? They paid you with gold, so it wasn't me they were running from.

RACHEL. They had to get away.

SIMON. From what? What had they done?

RACHEL. I didn't ask them, Simon. I didn't need to ask them. We've lived too long under Herod to start asking questions when people have to run away in the dark.

SIMON. But who could have warned him, in the middle of the night, like that? Did anybody come?

RACHEL. I never saw anybody.

SIMON. I'm sure they weren't planning to go yesterday.

RACHEL. I told them, "You'll never make it," I said. "There are soldiers everywhere, they always bring in extra troops at a time like this." I told them to leave it one more day, and it would be safer. But they wouldn't wait.

SIMON (*with compassion*) Fools. (*He comforts Rachel*) Ah, well, that wasn't your fault. You did your best, you warned them. I wonder what they'll do to them.

RACHEL (*half proud, half frightened*) They can't do anything to them. They're well away by now.

SIMON (*sharply*) How do you know?

Rachel. Because I took them, that's why. They'd never have made it on their own; they don't know the town, not where the troops are billeted, or—or anything. I carried the baby for them until they were clear out on to the Hebron road. There was no moon to speak of. And even that comet thing was fading by the time I came back. They'll be all right, now.

Simon (*terrified and angry*) Rachel! You must be out of your mind! You've *got* to *learn*, you—you can't *do* these things. What do you think they'd have done if they caught you?

Rachel. Well, they didn't, did they?

Simon. Oh, God, why do people like that have to come here? If I'd known they were that kind, I'd never have had anything to do with it. Who knows *what* they've done?

Rachel (*hotly*) If they've done anything to make Herod their enemy, then I'm glad I had the chance to help them. I'm sick and tired of holding my tongue.

Simon. And what do you think would happen to the business if they had the slightest suspicion of anything like that going on?

(Simon's *caution makes* Rachel *defiant. Her voice begins to ring*)

Rachel. If you want the truth, Simon, I *don't care* about the business. As long as we've got each other, and little David, there's nothing they can do to us that frightens me.

Simon. You talk like a child, Rachel. You don't seem to realize what Herod's capable of. He killed his own wife and his own sons —do you think he'd spare us?

Rachel (*stubbornly*) No, I don't suppose he would. But if they *did* find out, and killed the lot of us, at least we'd be all together. Even that might be better than crawling all our lives. (*She looks towards the manger. Softly*) What about *them?* They only had each other, didn't they—and I've never seen anybody look so happy.

Simon (*practical; discounting all this as ranting nonsense*) Do you think anyone saw you?

Rachel. No soldiers, anyway.

Simon (*impatiently*) But *anyone?*

Rachel (*scornfully*) No-one would tell *them* anything.

(Simon *makes* Rachel *look at him, despairing of making her realize*)

Simon. If that Joseph was important to them, they'll *make* people talk. Do you think it's only your own life you've been risking?

Rachel (*sobered*) I never thought of that.

Simon (*a little appeased at having communicated some of his fear*) That's the trouble with women, they never do think.

Rachel (*anxiously*) I don't *think* anyone saw us. Simon, wh-what are we going to do?

Simon. Easy to ask. That's the way these gestures of yours always end up, isn't it? "Simon, what are we going to do?" One thing we're *not* going to do, is pretend they weren't here. Too many people heard about it. Those shepherds saw them—what about that lamb the boy brought? Did they take that lamb with them?

Rachel. No, it's still here. (*She points up* L) I put it in the back stall—I was just trying to make it drink some milk. (*Nervously*) Shall I hide it? (*She looks around for a safe place*) What about the hay loft?

Simon. It's no good *hiding* anything. That would stamp us as liars right away. No. (*As if rehearsing for a statement*) They were here, but we didn't know who they were. That's the only way. We never even spoke to them—except to offer them a roof. We were too busy. (*Encouraged*) That's it! And—and they left in the night without paying—yes. Nobody saw them go. Well—(*he straightens himself, assuming more cheerfulness than he feels*) that's all we've got to tell them. We'll give them the lamb for their supper.

Rachel (*involuntarily*) Oh!

Simon. It wouldn't live without its mother, anyway. The boy was stupid to leave it here. Now, you know what to say? Keep out of their way if you can, but if they do ask you anything, you know what to say.

(Rachel, *chastened and a little nervous, goes to the door and opens it. Among the outdoor sounds admitted are the desultory whining of a baby, newly awakened, still drowsy, inclined to be hungry. And a more distant sound of drums, at first hardly more than a throbbing hum*)

(*He listens*) What's that?

Rachel (*smiling*) It's David woken up. He must be hungry, poor lamb.

Simon. No, not that. (*He motions Rachel to silence*)

(*They both listen. The sound of the drums gets louder*)

Come back. Shut the door a minute.

(Rachel *closes the door. The sound of the drums grows louder*)

Rachel. They're not coming here, Simon. (*It is not a statement, she is begging him to tell her that they are not*)

(Simon *beckons to* Rachel *who moves to him and clutches his arm. The drums grow louder. The lamb in the stall bleats. The drums grow still louder then the noise passes its peak and begins to grow less*)

(*Breathing it*) They're going past.

(SIMON *and* RACHEL *draw a little away from one another and look into each other's eyes as they listen*)

SIMON (*relaxing*) Yes.

(RACHEL *goes to the door, opens it and peers out*)

RACHEL. They've gone. They're stopping—they're stopping in the market-place.

(*The drums cease.* RACHEL, *light with relief, runs to the bench and picks up her head-scarf*)

SIMON (*clutching her arm*) Where are you going?
RACHEL. Down to see.
SIMON. Stay here!
RACHEL (*in a frenzy to get away*) Why? All the women are going. It was nothing to do with us. I want to know what it's all about.
SIMON (*reluctantly releasing her*) I thought you were going to feed the baby.

(*This almost holds* RACHEL)

RACHEL. Yes—but—I only want to find out what's happening. It won't hurt him to wait a few more minutes, will it? (*With fond scolding; proud of the baby's appetite*) He's too greedy, anyway. (*Her tone is coaxing*) Just to see what it's about, Simon.

(RACHEL *gives Simon no time to forbid it and slips out, closing the door behind her.* SIMON *waits a little, worried, in deep thought, then sighs, shakes his head and goes into the second stall*)

SIMON (*in the deep semi-intelligible talk of a farmer to his stock*) All right, then, boy, come up then, come on, boy . . .

(*From outside the terrible scream of a woman is heard. After a stunned silence, there are more screams and sobs and more and more hysterical cries of women, at some distance.* SIMON *comes out of the stall and waits, paralysed. The screams grow nearer. The door crashes open.* RACHEL *enters, her face transfixed with pity and horror*)

RACHEL. Simon—they . . . (*Her face works. She can find no words*)
SIMON. What's happening?

(RACHEL's *head shakes a fraction from side to side and she stretches out her arm to Simon*)

RACHEL. Simon, quick, they . . . (*Until now her pity has been for others. Now a new thought leaps into her eyes and brings a madness of terror. Without a sound her lips frame the name)* David!

Outside, the baby's whine changes suddenly to a bawl of outraged resentment and fright as if he had been too roughly picked up. The sound cuts out suddenly.

RACHEL *rushes out blindly, with a terrible tearing scream of "David! David! David!" dying into the distance.*

SIMON *follows her out as the* LIGHTS BLACK-OUT *and—*

the CURTAIN *falls*

SCENE II

SCENE—*The same. Late afternoon.*

When the CURTAIN *rises, the* OFFICER, *in uniform, is lying sprawled and motionless on the bench, his head at the left end. His neck is twisted awkwardly. His head and one arm, stained with blood, hang over the downstage side of the bench. The bucket from the bench lies on its side on the floor. The sack of grain at the end of the bench near his head has fallen over and some of its contents have spilled on to the ground.* RACHEL *enters, closes the door behind her and leans back against it. She does not see the Officer. Her face is tragic and stupefied, her movements heavy and numb. She moves a few paces forward along the wall* L, *supporting herself against it as though she can hardly stand, and then slides to the ground near the heap of hay and lies there, staring at nothing, and moaning.*

SIMON (*off; calling*) Rachel?

RACHEL (*thickly; not loudly enough for Simon to hear*) Go away.

(SIMON *enters*)

SIMON. Rachel? Oh—there you are. (*His voice is full of pity and concern. He goes to Rachel, lifts her gently to a sitting position and kneels beside her, supporting her*)

(RACHEL *looks at him, unresponding*)

Why don't you come in and lie down? If you don't want to see anybody, Martha will keep them out. Won't you? It's cold out here. You can't help David by . . .

(RACHEL'S *eyelids flicker once, but the rest of her face is stone*)

It—it was quick, you know. He can't have suffered much. Why don't you come in?

(RACHEL *shakes her head slightly*)

(*More urgently*) Come on, Rachel. At least let me put something around you. (*He rises and crosses to* L *to get an old cloak hanging on the wall. As he does so he sees the Officer and reacts sharply, with horror*) Rachel! Come here!

(RACHEL *rises and crosses to Simon. They stare at the Officer,* SIMON, *fearfully,* RACHEL *with indifference*)

God in Heaven! Who can have killed him?

RACHEL. Who is it?

SIMON. It's one of the soldiers.

RACHEL (*sharply*) Soldier?

SIMON. Yes. An officer, too. Gaulish, by the look of him.

(RACHEL *moves behind the bench and stands over the Officer, her stupor being replaced by an obsessive hatred. She grasps his hair and turns his face roughly towards her. It is the face of a man in his forties, a fair-haired, Celtic type, with skin now as pale as wax. There is no sign of life. She rolls his head back again with a spurning gesture*)

RACHEL. That's how I'd like to see every one of them.

(SIMON *looks around as if fearing she might be heard. He is very badly shaken*)

SIMON. For pity's sake, Rachel, don't talk like that. How did he get here? As if we hadn't got enough trouble already.

(RACHEL *shows no sign of hearing him. She is still not in her right mind. She remains glaring down at the Officer and suddenly bends over him with a paroxysm of hate contorting her face, and her fingers curved like talons. She buries both her hands in the Officer's grey curls and shakes him with insane violence, trying to beat his head against the bench*)

RACHEL (*through clenched teeth*) You killed him! You killed him! You killed my baby!

(SIMON, *appalled, pulls* RACHEL *away almost at once, against her violent resistance, and holds her tightly to him until her struggles cease, her rage turns to tears and her sobs subside a little. The outburst has done her a certain amount of good*)

SIMON (*patting her*) Sh—shhh! (*Gently*) You don't know that, Rachel. You never saw it done. He mightn't have been the one at all. Hush now.

(RACHEL *is quiet and exhausted*)

(*He goes on talking, partly to clear his own mind, partly that the sound of his voice might continue to soothe and distract Rachel from her passion to the necessity for planning*) You see, the thing is, Rachel—we've got to work out what's the best thing to do with him. I don't want him found here like that. Nobody'll believe it wasn't us that killed him. Look, sit here a minute, will you? (*He bends his head and looks into her eyes with anxious enquiry*)

(RACHEL's *lips are tremulous, but* SIMON *is satisfied that she is not going to rave again. He guides her to the milking stool* C, *where she sits*)

All right?

Rachel (*nodding*) I'm sorry.

(Simon *goes to the door and bars it*)

Simon. I don't want anyone coming in until I've made up my mind what to do. I wish I knew who'd done it. I wish I knew. I'll have to bury him. I don't see how it's going to be done, either. The place is alive with soldiers, and the ground as hard as iron. (*He turns from the door, sees something on the ground and picks it up*) Wait a minute!

Rachel. What is it?

Simon. Here's what killed him. (*He holds up a bloodstained knife*) But—this looks like one of *their* knives.

Rachel. Perhaps somebody killed him with his own knife.

Simon. Hasn't he got one, then? (*He crosses to* r *to examine the knife more closely in the light from the window*)

(Rachel *rises, goes to the Officer and without compunction, rolls him over and takes out the knife from his belt*)

Rachel. Yes. His is still here. Look. (*She crosses to Simon and gives him the knife*)

(*The* Officer's *eyelids flicker. He opens his eyes and tries to lift his head, but a twinge of pain crosses his face. His lips part as if he would groan or cry out, but his head falls back again without his having uttered a sound. Neither* Rachel *nor* Simon *has noticed*)

Simon (*comparing the knives*) You see? The same. One of his own side must have done it, then.

Rachel. Why would they kill him?

Simon. Perhaps they didn't like what they were being asked to do.

Rachel (*violently*) Like it? *Like it?*

Simon (*taken aback by the violence of her reaction*) I mean, perhaps they . . .

Rachel. You talk about them as if they were *men*, as if they had ordinary human feelings. (*The storm has burst at last. She is loud, bitter, voluble, grief and hate tumbling out together*) What sort of *men*, what sort of *soldiers*, would do a thing like that? Little babies, little helpless babies, what harm had they ever done, what harm could they do? (*Her tears stream down*) Our David couldn't even sit up by himself. Only yesterday, I saw him trying to lift his little head. If there'd been a real man among the lot of them, he'd have stuck a knife in Herod there and then, when he gave the order, not left it till they were here, and it was all over, and too late.

Simon. All the same—there was a bit of a fight between some of them. I heard them talking about it. It was over Esther's baby.

Rachel. *Esther's* baby? The new one?

Simon. Yes.

Rachel (*with horror*) But—I thought it—they were saying yesterday it was—it had been born—with . . .

Simon. That's right. That's why some of them said there was no point in killing it. "It's got no arms," they said. She was lying over the top of it—screaming—they couldn't pull her off. Of course she feels the same about it as if it had been—like any other. One of the officers told them they could leave it. It couldn't possibly be this one, they said, look at it, it couldn't possibly. But the other one said, "The orders were all of them. Let it be all of them."

Rachel. So—what happened?

Simon. Oh, I don't know. One or two of the soldiers started shouting. It's been pretty edgy with them all day; they had to let some of them get drunk to make them go through with it at all. Anyway, there was a bit of a fight. You couldn't call it a mutiny, exactly.

Rachel (*impatiently*) I mean the baby? What happened?

Simon. Well, nothing. They forgot about it, I suppose. They had to try and deal with the soldiers.

Rachel. So—that's the only one left. (*Bitterly*) And we'd all been so sorry for Esther when it was born like that. Lucky, lucky Esther. And that other one, that carpenter's wife! Mary—she's all right, too, isn't she? She got away just in time. I'd like to know how she's different from the rest of us, that she's allowed to go all through her life with no sorrows to face.

(*Footsteps and some drunken singing are heard outside the door.* Simon *is galvanized*)

Simon. I'd better not stay here too long.

Voice (*off; calling*) Landlord!

Simon (*calling*) Coming, sir. (*To Rachel*) Look, you'd better stay here. If anybody comes, get rid of them somehow. I won't be longer than I can help. I can't do much with him till it gets dark. (*He puts the Officer's knife on the stool and conceals the bloodstained knife in his clothes*)

Voice (*off; calling*) Landlord! Landlord!

Simon (*moving to the door and unbarring it*) See if you can hide him. Try and get him over by the wall, and cover him over, just for now. (*He opens the door and calls*) All right, all right.

(Simon *exits, closing the door behind him.* Rachel *bars the door then first tries to drag the bench to the wall* l, *but it is too heavy for her in her state of exhaustion. She looks at the Officer, wondering whether she can carry him, but she is breathing heavily and wipes her brow with a trembling hand. She decides she can only cover him where he lies and collects a pile of hay from the corner down* r. *While she is there the*

B

OFFICER *groans and gives a weak, dry cough. His eyes are still closed.*
RACHEL *drops the hay and crosses swiftly to him*)

RACHEL. You're alive! (*With vindictive intensity*) I'm glad. (*From this point on, her whole being centres on the Officer with an avid concentration. She can hardly take her eyes off him. She is unwilling to miss a single word that he speaks. She wants to force him to as acute an awareness of herself. She is tied to him with a bond as strong and relentless as physical passion, but there is not at any time an atom of sex in it. The passion that consumes her is hatred*) Tell me, are you proud of yourself?

(*The* OFFICER *licks his lips and tries dazedly to open his eyes*)

(*Passionately*) Answer me.

(*The* OFFICER *opens his mouth, but all that comes out again is the weak dry cough*)

(*Half to herself, aware that he is not taking much in*) You're going to answer me, you know. Oh, yes. You're going to answer. (*She takes some sacks and piles them on to the end of the bench for the Officer to lean against and pulls him up into a sitting position so that she can see him better. She pours a beaker of water from a jar on the shelf* L *and gives him a drink, not as an act of mercy but as a lever to force words out of him*)

(*The* OFFICER *is not aware of her mood. He drinks and furrows his brow with concentration, scarcely glancing at her. He is a man without formal education, but with intelligence, experience, and a serviceable understanding of the world*)

OFFICER. How long have I been here?

(RACHEL *gives the Officer a curious thin smile. He has not yet seen his danger and she will play with him a little. She keeps menace out of her voice and answers smoothly*)

RACHEL. Half a day, soldier.
OFFICER (*impatient of the weakness in himself*) I don't seem to remember what happened.
RACHEL. No, that's easy to see.

(*The* OFFICER *glances sharply at her, but to deduce rather than ask*)

OFFICER. So the Jews kicked at last, did they? I've seen it coming. But I never thought they'd really have the guts. How many of us are left?
RACHEL. I don't know.
OFFICER. Did you bring me here?
RACHEL. No. I found you here.
OFFICER. Oh. (*He pauses. Thoughtfully*) That was a bit of luck.
RACHEL. Why?

OFFICER. Well—if any of your *men* had found me in this state, I wouldn't give much for my chances. They must have gone pretty berserk to have attacked us at all. (*He looks warily at her*) You—you're not going to fetch anybody, are you?

(RACHEL *is silent*)

(*His eyes grow anxious*) It wouldn't be a pretty thing for a woman to watch.

RACHEL (*softly*) Oh, no. I won't fetch anybody.

OFFICER. That's all right, then.

RACHEL. Not for the world.

OFFICER. I'll make it worth your while. Just let me stay here till things die down a bit and I can get away. (*He puts a hand up to explore his wound, and his anxiety returns*) It may not be for three or four days. Do you think you can manage that long?

RACHEL (*smiling*) I don't think you'll be here as long as that.

OFFICER. I'm not so sure. I feel very—(*his voice and his eyes falter*) as if . . . (*He closes his eyes and takes two deep breaths to master a momentary panic*) I suppose I've lost a lot of blood. I still can't remember what happened.

RACHEL. Do you remember what town this is?

OFFICER. No.

RACHEL (*pouncing at last*) That's where you made your mistake. You think it's like all the other places where you've been doing Herod's dirty work for him. A bad mistake, soldier. This place is different.

(*The* OFFICER, *taken aback at Rachel's change of tone, looks uncomprehendingly at her*)

A piece of luck, you said, that it was a woman who found you. Oh, yes. I'm aware you and your kind have always found it so. Women are poor soft things, aren't they? Their hearts are soft and yielding, like their breasts, aren't they? (*From irony, her voice suddenly grows harsh and ugly with naked hate*) But this is *Bethlehem*, soldier. Does that mean anything to you? (*She clasps her breasts and rocks to and fro in anguish*) Do you see these breasts? *They* aren't soft and yielding. No! They're hard and hurting, and everything inside me is the same, and in every street in Bethlehem tonight there's a woman like me. Do you want to know why they're like this? Because *my baby is dead*. He's dead. Eight hours ago I heard him crying in his cot, crying to be fed, crying for me. And my body was calling for him as his was calling for me. (*Her agony flows over her. She weeps, throws her head back and cries to David*) And I was coming, I *was*, I swear I was coming to you, pet. (*Her face contorts and she thrusts it at the Officer*) But somebody got there before me. Do you remember any of that? I'm going to make sure you do remember before you

die. You'll remember what Bethlehem means. It's the place where
any soldier waking wounded would have a different prayer on his
lips for once, and say, "Oh, God of mercy, let it be a *man* that finds
me here."

OFFICER (*still and quiet*) Yes, I remember now.

RACHEL. You'd better remember. Because now you're going to
tell me.

OFFICER. Tell you what?

RACHEL. I want to know what goes on inside you, I want to
know what shapes you've got to twist your mind into, to make you
able to do things like that.

OFFICER (*turning his head away and frowning with impatience*) Do you
think I enjoyed it?

RACHEL (*bitterly*) Didn't you?

OFFICER (*glaring hotly at her*) I had no choice. It was part of my
job. It's not a thing a woman can be expected to understand.

RACHEL. No? They can be expected to bear the children,
though, and feed them to your swords and into your armies,
generation after generation. We don't need to understand, do we?
Because it's the men that hold the weapons. But just this once it
isn't. (*She picks up the Officer's knife from the stool*) Now. Make me
understand. (*She puts the knife near the Officer's throat*) Make me understand why it wasn't filthy murder.

(*The* OFFICER *is silent*)

(*She advances the blade till it touches his skin*) Talk!

(*The* OFFICER *is silent*)

(*She sets her lips and presses until the point of the knife, though not breaking
the skin, dents deep into his neck*) Go on, talk! What are you waiting
for?

OFFICER (*keeping very still; without emotion*) A little farther to
the right would make a better job of it. Quicker. And not so
messy.

(RACHEL *slowly relaxes and lowers the knife*)

Aren't you going to do it?

RACHEL. Not like that. It's too good for you. You're not going
out with that smug look on your face, thinking you've done something dutiful and heroic. Did you do any of it yourself, or only tell
your soldiers to? Did you watch it going on? Would you like me to
go and fetch David's body and show it to you? Or would that
make you prouder still of yourself to see the enemy you've been
men enough to kill, you and a couple of dozen others, your terrible
enemy nearly five weeks old? (*A despairing grief overcomes her again at*

the thought of David. She sinks down to the ground beside the bench and buries her face in the hay)

(*The* Officer *is made far more uneasy by her tears than her threats*)

Officer (*wearily*) It wasn't my choice. I had no choice. It was part of my job.

Rachel. Do you have to do everything they tell you? What are you, then, a slave?

Officer. You can't have an army if your men are going to examine every order and refuse it if it happens to be—unpleasant.

Rachel. I believe you're proud of going through with it.

Officer. Somebody had to do it.

Rachel. Why?

Officer. Listen! You don't think you're going to get away with this, do you? I remember it all, now, and we haven't been wiped out at all. It wasn't even an uprising. It was only two men, and our men at that. Do you think I don't remember? How long do you think it'll be before someone comes to find me? What do you imagine will happen to you, then?

(Rachel *laughs, a terrible laugh compounded of suffering and almost pitying incredulity*)

Rachel (*passionately*) Do you think I care what happens to me now?

(*The* Officer's *expression changes. His eyes grow wary. For the first time he feels in immediate danger from her*)

Officer (*slowly*) I think you're mad.

Rachel. Oh, yes! Oh, yes, that must be it. And that frightens you, doesn't it? Good! (*She settles near him again*) So now—you'll tell me.

(*The* Officer *licks his lips*)

Officer (*stalling and humouring her*) I told you. There's nothing to say. It was part of the job.

Rachel. Job? What kind of job is that? How can men turn themselves into hired killers for a madman like Herod?

Officer. Well, he—(*he speaks automatically, unable to think clearly, his eyes fearfully on the knife in Rachel's hand*) I mean, he's trying to put the country on its feet, isn't he? And he's got a lot of enemies, he's got to protect himself—people don't always know what's good for them, do they?

Rachel (*harshly*) And Herod does?

Officer (*recoiling*) No, I—I'm not saying that, exactly. But he . . . (*He hesitates*)

Rachel. He what?

Officer. Well, you know what it was like before, don't you? Ask your mother, she'll tell you. (*He gains confidence very slightly*) Fighting all the time, civil war, everybody at each other's throats. Say what you like about Herod, he's kept the peace for you, hasn't he? Isn't that worth something?

Rachel (*wildly; as though one or other of them must indeed be mad*) Peace! God in Heaven, listen to him! Peace!

(*The* Officer *leans back, trembling, shrugs and throws up his hand on his unwounded side, conveying the end of an effort he always knew to be fruitless*)

No. Go on.

(*The* Officer *shakes his head, coughs, closes his eyes and wipes his forehead with a shaky hand. Fear has drained his strength*)

(*She puts down the knife, rises, picks up the beaker, goes into the stall* L *and brings him some ass's milk*) Here. Here's some milk.

(*The* Officer *sips the milk*)

Go on.

(*The* Officer *drinks, wipes his mouth and revives a little*)

(*She resumes relentlessly*) Go on—you were saying—"Peace . . ."

Officer. It's no use. Look—what do you expect me to say?

Rachel. I want to know what you're doing here, don't you see? I've got to *know*. I can't bear it being such a *senseless* thing, no point in it, no reason for it. Why couldn't you have stayed in your own country and left us alone? And why *Bethlehem* of *all* places?

Officer. All right, then. If that's what you want to know, I'll tell you. There was a rumour about a royal baby being born here. Some travelling fakirs came and told Herod about it. A prince. Don't you see what that means? A pretender to the throne. What would you *expect* him to do about it?

Rachel (*bewildered*) But that's—that's just silly. You don't get princes born in little places like this.

Officer. I don't suppose you do. But it wouldn't have mattered if it was true or false, as long as enough people had believed it. There's plenty of people only looking for an excuse to stir up trouble against Herod. This would have been just what they wanted. They'd have lined up half the country behind this—this kid, whoever he was. You'd have had civil war again in no time. You'd have been right back where you were.

(*The news has diverted* Rachel's *thoughts and she speaks more quietly, not looking at him. The* Officer, *in his turn, grows more urgently reasonable, with renewed hopes of breaking her obsession*)

Rachel. Who told you all this?

Officer. In Jerusalem everybody was full of it. So you see, he's got to do something, hasn't he? He's got to put a stop to it, I mean. Of course, it seems cruel, of *course* it does—but—it's a deterrent. That's all it is.

Rachel (*slowly*) A what?

Officer. You don't think anybody *wants* to use these methods, do you? But it's the only way if he's going to get the country settled, and—and civilized. He's got to show people that they can't get away with that sort of thing. It may save thousands of lives in the long run.

Rachel (*in a desperate voice*) You say these *words!* Men say all these words to themselves, they fill their minds with a smoke of words so that they shan't see what they're doing. Peace—civilization—but what have you *done?* What you have done is to empty every cradle in Bethlehem except one. And that's the future you're fighting to defend? All the babies dead except the poor little mismade things?

Officer. I keep telling you, we didn't want to do that. If your people had been a little bit more co-operative we wouldn't have had to. There was only one that Herod wanted. If that one had been just quietly handed over, none of this would have been necessary. Just a word or a hint would have been enough—but, oh, no. Not the Jews. Not a word out of any of them—*they* knew nothing of any prince.

Rachel (*with a terrible realization*) You're saying if you caught that baby, all the others would have lived? David, too?

Officer. Exactly—that's the whole point. Even now I've got a feeling that he wasn't among them.

Rachel. No, he wasn't.

Officer. So he *did* get away?

Rachel. Yes. He got away.

Officer (*bitterly*) I knew it. And they covered up for him. Well, maybe now you understand it better. If you want to hate somebody, go and find out who helped them to escape. That's the one who's responsible for all this.

Rachel. I don't have to find out, soldier. I know who it was.

Officer. Good. (*He points to the knife*) Then you know who to use that knife on.

Rachel (*picking up the knife; slowly*) I'll know enough never to do a kind thing for anybody again, if this is how God punishes an act of mercy. It's a very valuable lesson, soldier. But you are the last one who should have driven it home.

(*There is a knock at the door*)

Rachel (*calling*) Simon?

Simon (*off*) Yes.

(RACHEL *turns to go to the door, stops as a thought strikes her, hides the knife under the hay down* R, *then goes to the door and opens it.*
SIMON *enters*)

Where is he?

(RACHEL *nods towards the bench*)

(*He looks at the bench, his hand still on the latch as he closes the door, but from where he is he can only see the Officer's feet. He frowns*) I told you to cover him up.

RACHEL. Time enough for that when he's dead.

(SIMON *stares at Rachel, crosses to the bench and is stunned to see the* OFFICER *alive and looking at him*)

It's not often we have a chance of entertaining such a distinguished guest. He's been telling me about "Peace". And "Honour", Simon. And "Duty", and a lot of other fine manly reasons for killing babies in their mothers' arms.

SIMON (*stooping down beside the Officer*) Oh, the Lord be praised, sir. We thought you were dead. I've been in terror of my life. I knew if they found you here they'd never believe we had no part in it. Now you can tell them. Now you can testify. Are you badly hurt, sir? Rachel, quick, go and get some wine—the best—and bring it here right away. And tell Martha to get a bed ready, and warm some oil.

(RACHEL *does not move*)

What are you waiting for?

RACHEL (*looking at Simon with cold repressed contempt*) Nothing.

(RACHEL *exits, closing the door behind her*)

SIMON. You'll be well cared for, sir, believe me. If anybody asks, you can tell them that. My wife shall wait on you with her own hands. She's an excellent nurse, sir. She has a very gentle touch.

OFFICER. I can imagine.

SIMON (*with enthusiasm*) Oh, it's true, sir. You ought to see her with the ch-child . . . (*He has stumbled over the word, realized it too late to withdraw it and gives himself a new angle on it so that the memory shall not spoil his satisfaction at this new development*) Besides, it will occupy her time. It will help to take her mind off things. That's just what she needs most, just now, a task to dedicate herself to.

OFFICER. I think she's found one.

SIMON. Do you know the ones who did it, sir?

OFFICER (*putting a hand up to his shoulder*) I might recognize them. I'm not sure. There were only two of them.

SIMON. But it *was* soldiers, sir? It wasn't any of us?

OFFICER. No, it wasn't the Jews this time.

SIMON. That's all right, then. (*Anxiously*) I wish she'd hurry with the wine.

OFFICER. My life is precious to you, landlord.

SIMON (*nervously and confidentially*) The thing is, the people have had just about all they can stand already. The women, sir, it's— you can't imagine what it's like in the town—they're clean out of their minds, some of them. It makes it a terrible time for everybody, with the women like that. So I mean—if you were to die, and nobody could prove it wasn't a Jew that did it, then they might start on us again, and I don't know what would happen. We're a people that will put up with an awful lot. You know that. But today has been just about enough.

OFFICER. You might mention to your wife how much hangs on my survival.

SIMON (*deprecatingly*) Oh, women don't understand these things, sir. Their minds don't work like ours; they think with their nerves. But she'll do what I tell her, don't you worry.

OFFICER. Will she?

(RACHEL *enters, carrying a flagon of wine and a beaker*)

SIMON. Bring it here.

(RACHEL, *wordless and expressionless, moves to the bench, pours some wine and holds it out. The* OFFICER *takes the beaker, lifts it to his lips, lowers it and looks at* RACHEL *who returns his gaze unblinking*)

OFFICER (*as though, having sniffed the wine, he is questioning its quality*) Did you say your *best* wine, landlord?

SIMON (*fussily*) Where did you get it from, Rachel? Let me try it. (*He holds out his hand for the flagon*)

(*The* OFFICER *watches them both closely.* RACHEL *reads his mind and gives a slow scornful smile*)

RACHEL (*deliberately*) Of course, if you want to, Simon. (*She hands him the flagon*)

(SIMON *tastes the wine and nods*)

SIMON (*with only slight professional anxiety*) It's the best vintage we have. I think you'll find it to your liking.

RACHEL. Perhaps he doesn't like drinking alone.

(*The* OFFICER *drinks*)

SIMON. Is it all right?

OFFICER. It's excellent.

SIMON (*to Rachel*) Is the bed ready?

RACHEL. Yes.

Simon. Good, good. (*He puts the flagon on the shelf* l) I was telling the Officer you'll take good care of him.

Rachel. It will be a pleasure. He knows that.

Simon. Now, sir, if you could put that arm around me here— you'll be warmer inside, and much more comfortable—and the women will see to your shoulder.

(*The* Officer, *with Simon's assistance, tries to get to his feet, but the pain is too great*)

Officer. No. No, I can't. It's no good. Tomorrow, maybe. (*He claps a hand to the wound high on his back, and brings it round to the front covered with blood. He sinks back slowly*)

Simon (*aghast*) Rachel! Quick!

(Rachel *moves without haste and surveys the Officer's wound without pity*)

Rachel. It's nothing much. You were too rough with him. See, it's stopping.

Simon. He's gone white, hasn't he?

Rachel. He lost a lot before.

Simon (*to the Officer*) Are you all right?

Officer (*testily*) Yes. Yes, yes.

Simon (*to Rachel*) I wonder what we'd better do?

Officer. What's happening out there? Are the people quiet?

Simon (*with restrained resentment*) There's nothing much they can do, is there? Two or three of them tried to stop it. It only left their wives with two to bury instead of one.

Officer. And the troops?

Simon (*shrugging*) They're still there. Seemed to me they didn't quite know what they were supposed to be doing. Some of them are still searching the houses. (*With the nearest he comes to overt bitterness*) They won't find any more babies, if that's what they're looking for.

Officer. What do you think they're looking for? They're looking for me.

Simon. So you'd be the captain, then, sir?

Officer. You'd better go and fetch one of them. Tell him where I am. The lieutenant, if you can find him.

Simon. Yes. Yes, of course, sir, right away. (*He hesitates*) Where would he be?

Officer (*testily*) I tell you I don't know. This operation has been a shambles from the beginning. Go and look for him, man. Ask somebody.

Simon. Yes. I'll do that. (*He moves to the door, stops and turns*) Rachel.

Rachel. What?

Simon. Don't leave him, will you?
Rachel. No fear of that, Simon.
Simon. For pity's sake don't let anything happen to him, now.
Rachel. Go on, Simon.

(Simon *exits*)

(*She closes the door after him and leans against it with a half-mad laugh*)
For pity's sake! Pity, for the murderers. Pity, for the butchers.
Pity for the bullies and the thugs. Never mind the children and
their little mangled bodies, never mind the girls and women
with their lives in ruins. Pity, pity for the monsters and the cowards
that did it to them! There's been too much of that kind of pity.
(*She gets the knife from its hiding-place*) Look! (*She holds up the knife*) It's
my turn now to do a little deterring. (*She looks over her shoulder as
if to make sure Simon has gone*) He's a coward, too. He knows what it
says in the Holy Book—"An eye for an eye, a life for a life". But
all he thinks about is his own skin. Pity! He knows what you've
done and he still thinks I'm going to have pity on you. He must
be out of his mind. The world's been going on a long, long time,
but I never heard of anybody yet who said we ought to forgive
our enemies. (*She takes a step or two towards the Officer*)
Officer. You're not going to use that thing.
Rachel. What's going to stop me?
Officer. What do you think you'll gain by that?
Rachel. I've got nothing to gain. But I've got nothing to lose
now, either. And some time or other people like you have got to be
stopped.
Officer. You'll never do it. Not now. Not in cold blood.
Rachel. Do you think it cools so quickly? Haven't you realized
yet what it is you've done? Wait, then. I'll show you. I'll bring
him to you. I wouldn't want you to die without knowing why.

(Rachel *puts the knife on the stool and exits quickly. The* Officer
*waits a moment to be sure she has really gone, then painfully rolls over
on to his side and looks at the knife on the stool, out of his reach. By
stretching his arm to its fullest extent he manages with difficulty to grasp
the handle of a light wooden rake leaning against the wall behind him.
He tries to use it to drag the stool towards him, but he is weak, and he
soon has to stop to recover his breath. Hearing a step outside he makes
another desperate effort, but he is clumsy in his haste and knocks the stool
over. He groans in despair as the door opens.*
    The Soldier *enters. He is dirty, unshaven, dishevelled, slightly
tipsy and unsteady in his gait. He holds a bottle of wine*)

Officer. Bar the door.
Soldier. You're alive, then.
Officer. Bar the door.

SOLDIER (*barring the door*) What for?

OFFICER. She's coming back.

SOLDIER. That girl that went out?

OFFICER. Yes.

SOLDIER (*with a tipsy laugh*) And you want to stop her? I wish I had half your trouble. Locking her in, I'd be, not out.

OFFICER. She's gone out to get her baby.

SOLDIER (*his face darkening*) Baby? Baby? (*Bitterly*) Did we miss one, then?

OFFICER. No, it's dead. She thinks I killed it.

SOLDIER. Did you?

OFFICER. How do I know? They all look alike to me.

SOLDIER. What's she fetching it for if it's dead?

OFFICER. Because she's mad.

SOLDIER. Oh, I see. I saw another the same half a mile back. Been dead for hours, hers had, and they couldn't get her to leave go of it. Talkin' to it an' that.

OFFICER. She wants to show it to me, she says she wants it to be the last thing I see in this world. But that's not why she's fetching it. She's fetching it to work herself up. She's finding it's not as easy as she thinks, to kill a man. She might just manage it if she's got that in front of her.

SOLDIER. Wants to finish you off, does she?

OFFICER. Yes.

SOLDIER (*reasonably*) Mmm! Well, you can't hardly blame her, can you? (*He drinks from his bottle*) Want some of this?

(*The* OFFICER *drinks some wine. The* SOLDIER *makes some effort to make the Officer comfortable. He offers some food, too, which the* OFFICER *holds in his hand at first, but eats a little later when the wine takes effect*)

OFFICER. Where have I seen you before?

SOLDIER (*grinning and shaking his head*) Must be a wonderful thing, being an officer. (*The grin fades and he speaks accusingly with a touch of hurt and resentment*) I been serving under you for five years. I s'pose all of us look the same to you, too, like the Jew babies. Just a lot of faces. I thought you might have remembered this one, though.

OFFICER (*coldly*) It's a wonder I recognized you as a soldier at all. How did you get yourself into that state? It's disgusting. Pull yourself together, man.

SOLDIER. Marvellous, i'n't it! Only two swallows and he's back on his charger dishin' out orders. (*He shakes his head*) It's no good, you know. I'm packin' it in.

OFFICER. You mean you're deserting?

SOLDIER. Not that I've got any option. I'm thinkin' of others that's all. I'm savin' the rest of the boys the job of having to put me to death. They've had enough dirty work to do without me on top of it.

OFFICER. Death?

SOLDIER. That's what you get, isn't it?

OFFICER. For what?

SOLDIER. Mutiny?

OFFICER. So that's where I've seen you.

SOLDIER. That's right.

OFFICER. What happened to the other one?

SOLDIER. Run for it, of course. Did a bit of lootin' on the way so he could hire a boat, and pinched a donkey to get him to the coast. He must be half-way there by now. Makin' for—well, it's nothing to do with you where he's making for.

(*There is a knock at the door*)

(*He calls*) Who's that?

(*The knocking stops*)

Is that you, my pretty?

RACHEL (*off*) Who's there?

OFFICER. You're not going to let her in?

SOLDIER. Now, why should I leave her standing out there? You can't keep a woman out of her own stable.

OFFICER. I told you—she's out of her mind.

SOLDIER. She's not the only one. There's a few of our chaps pretty near the edge, and that's a fact.

OFFICER (*suspiciously*) Perhaps you're on the same side as she is? Is that what you came back for—to finish what you started?

SOLDIER (*pointing an outstretched finger at the Officer; defiantly*) I had my bellyful of that business this morning, I can tell you that.

(*There is a harder knocking on the door*)

(*He calls*) All right, all right, don't batter the door down. (*He goes to the door and opens it*)

(RACHEL, *holding David's body, hesitates on the threshold*)

Come on in, lady. It's cold out there. (*He puts out his hand, draws Rachel gently inside and shuts the door*) Is that your little one? (*He takes the body from her*)

(RACHEL *stares at the Soldier as if hypnotized, and makes no resistance*)

(*He feels the child's rigor*) Ah. Poor little devil. Stiff as marble. (*With one hand he pushes back the wrappings to look at the face and speaks even more gently and with wonder*) But I never saw anything carved so perfect as this. (*To Rachel*) A boy?

(RACHEL *nods, her eyes welling in response to his compassion*)

He was beautiful all right.

(RACHEL *draws in a shuddering breath*)

(*He puts his free arm around Rachel in a gesture of rough comfort*) There's only one thing wrong with boys, my dear. They grow into men. (*Suddenly; in mild disgust at life or himself*) Here, take him. I've forgotten how to hold them. (*He hands the body to Rachel*) What is it you want?

(RACHEL *stares at him*)

Well, you must have come for something?

RACHEL (*pointing at the Officer; hardening*) He's the one that did it.

SOLDIER. How do you know?

RACHEL. He doesn't even deny it.

SOLDIER. He can't, because he doesn't know. None of us know. It might have—(*he stops and looks at David's body in a kind of fear*) it might have been . . . (*He drinks from his bottle, throws back his head and cries in desperation*) What's the matter with the wine in this place? I've drunk enough to sink a ship. (*He controls himself and speaks in a flat voice, hard and uncompromising, but without meeting Rachel's eyes*) It might have been me, lady.

RACHEL. You?

SOLDIER (*tormented*) You don't think we look at their faces? That's the way we fight these days, you know, that's the modern way. If you can't get at the guilty, kill the innocent. Women and children. People who can't hit back. So they make it easier for us, see—we don't have to look them in the eyes.

RACHEL. I don't believe it was you.

SOLDIER (*looking dully at her*) I wonder why not. Because you want to even that score, and I look too big and healthy to be snuffed out easily? You don't want to let that worry you. I'm not seeing any too well, as a matter of fact, and I've been sick in my stomach all day. I won't put up much of a fight. (*He pulls at the neck of his tunic trying to bare his breast, and spreads his arms wide*) Come on.

RACHEL (*uneasily*) I don't care who did it. *He* was giving the orders.

SOLDIER. True. But—he was taking them, too, remember.

RACHEL. Oh, why did *you* have to come? It was hard enough before. Are you the one that Simon was to fetch?

SOLDIER. Who's that?

RACHEL. Are you the lieutenant?

(*The* Soldier *laughs and looks to the Officer to share the joke*)

Soldier. Hah! There's promotion for you.

Rachel. Well, who *did* send you, then? Who sent you? Tell me!

(*The* Officer *closes his eyes and then remains motionless*)

Soldier. I came to see if he was alive or dead.

Rachel. How did you know where to come?

Soldier. Because this was where we left him.

Rachel (*her face slowly growing radiant*) I knew it. I knew you were a good man.

Soldier (*his mouth twisting, tasting the unfamiliar word*) Good?

Rachel (*her words flooding out with relief and urgency*) Simon told me about the mutiny. You did it, didn't you? You tried to kill him and put an end to the bloodshed and save the children. *You* could see how wicked it was. (*She picks up the knife and presents it, handle first, to the Soldier*) Here. Finish it now, then. Finish it for us. And—and I'll tell everybody in the town. And none of them will ever forget you—they'll always remember that even in Herod's army there are *some* men with—hearts—and consciences.

Soldier (*backing away from the knife*) Take it away.

Rachel. Please! It's not a woman's job.

(*The* Soldier *backs to the door and almost cringes*)

Soldier (*shouting*) Take it away, I tell you! Take it away.

Rachel. But he's the one responsible. He's a murderer.

Soldier (*sweating*) And what are you tryin' to make me?

Rachel. This wouldn't be murder, this would be justice.

Soldier (*still taut; his eyes as fascinated on the knife as if it had been presented point first at his heart*) That's only a word, lady, it's only a word.

Rachel (*holding the knife higher to him*) But you . . .

Soldier (*with menace; loudly*) Look, I'm tellin' you, don't keep on at me, don't keep shovin' it under my nose. That's what we turned on him for. We'd had enough.

(Rachel *looks at the Soldier with growing scorn and finally lowers the knife*)

(*Trembling*) That's better. Drop it down a well or something. (*He holds out his hand*) Give it here, let's get rid of it.

(Rachel *puts the knife behind her back*)

(*He mops his brow*) I'm sorry, lady. Don't look at me like that. It was you made out I was some kind of hero, I never said so. Hearts and consciences and all that, they never came into it. It was just my stomach turned weak on me. The whole thing made me want to heave. The women—screamin' and yellin' and hangin' on to our knees; you couldn't move a step without kickin' them loose, and—you could—smell the terror in them. The—the little —the little—(*his face twists*) their bodies were too soft, you know, the blade goes in too easy, it feels all wrong, disgusting, like maggots. (*He gives a kind of sob, then with an effort regains control and continues quietly*) I wouldn't have thought it would have turned me up like that, though. I think it must have been the wine, as well. (*He looks accusingly at the bottle in his hand*) I don't know what vintage you got in Bethlehem this year, there's somethin' funny about it—cloudy —as if it's been mixed with milk. (*He sets the stool upright, sits on it and looks at the Officer*) Even him, see. I could have been clear away —but I kept thinkin', "What if he's still alive and the Jews get hold of him, the state they're in, what'll they do to him?" I had to come back and see. He don't remember me, but he got me out of a terrible tight spot once. Few years back—up in the mountains. (*With nostalgia*) Good, clean fightin'.

(*There is silence for a moment*)

(*He rises*) It's getting dark. Shall I light the lamp? (*He puts down his bottle*)

RACHEL (*expressionless*) Yes. Light it.

(*The SOLDIER gets a lamp from the shelf L, lights it and puts it on a ledge R, just above and behind the manger, so that it shines on and illuminates the fresh hay. RACHEL drops the knife, sits on the stool and rocks her baby, her face blank and mindless*)

SOLDIER (*moving to Rachel*) You can do him no good any more.

(*RACHEL clutches the baby tighter*)

It will be better if you let him go.

(*RACHEL looks with hostility at the Soldier and remains silent*)

Look. (*He turns back the wrappings and shows her the baby's face*) Do you think he would want you to use him just to work up your hate with?

(*At the sight of David's face, pity and love flood through RACHEL again and turn her limbs to water and her resentment to pure grief. The SOLDIER gently takes the baby. RACHEL covers her face with her hands and rocks herself in an agony of bereavement. The SOLDIER puts the baby in the manger. The woollen wrapping is haloed in the lamplight*)

He'll be all right there.

RACHEL (*looking up; thickly*) That's where the other one was.

SOLDIER. Which one was that?

RACHEL. No-one will ever bring gold and perfume to mine.

SOLDIER (*looking down at the manger*) I've got no gold, son. It's too far from pay-day. (*He takes out a coin and drops it in the manger*) But here's a little piece of silver. And the hay smells nicer than any old scent. You could almost swear it was—still warm. (*He turns*) Now, then. (*He brushes from his fingers the chaff-dust and the feel of death, and crosses to the Officer*) What are we going to do about you? (*He looks at the wound*) Oh, Jupiter! (*He looks away, swallows and wipes his brow*) Did I do that? (*He breathes hard for a moment*) He's in a bit of a mess here, lady, isn't he? Have you got anything you could put on it?

RACHEL (*with the same expressionless answers she had given to Simon*) Inside.

SOLDIER. Go and fetch it, will you? (*He waits, his eyes on her, for a response*)

(RACHEL *slowly rises*)

(*He turns to the Officer, satisfied*) And some water, to clean him up a bit. And a drink.

RACHEL (*pointing to the flagon*) There's wine there.

(*The* SOLDIER *picks up the flagon and shakes it*)

SOLDIER. Don't be too long. (*He turns to the Officer*) I think he's passed out.

(RACHEL, *instead of going out as bidden, sinks down beside the manger and rests her head against it, worshipping and mourning the body of her child*)

OFFICER (*opening his eyes*) No. I'm all right.

SOLDIER (*turning to Rachel*) Go on, then. (*He crosses to her. Crossly*) Look, will you go now?

(RACHEL *looks up in silence*)

(*He pulls Rachel to her feet*) Go, when I'm askin' you. You'll have plenty of time for cryin' some other day. But he's in a bad way.

(RACHEL *looks stonily from the Soldier to the Officer then exits without haste, leaving the door open. It is now dark outside*)

OFFICER. The door . . .

SOLDIER. Never mind the door. She can't hurt you while I'm here.

OFFICER. If she thought that, she wouldn't come back at all.

SOLDIER. She'll come back. (*He nods towards the manger*) She can't keep away from that.

OFFICER. She's dangerous. Her mind is deranged.

SOLDIER (*soothingly*) Yes, well, it was the shock. She'll come round. (*He gives the flagon to the Officer*) Here.

C

Officer (*curiously*) Why did you really come back? (*He drinks*)

(*The* Soldier *gives a slight, rather silly laugh, having given up trying to understand himself*)

Soldier. I must have been drunk. (*He takes the flagon*) That better? (*He puts the flagon on the shelf* L)

(*The* Officer *nods*)

Who's this Simon she talked about?

Officer. Her husband. The innkeeper. I sent him with a message.

Soldier. Will he take it?

Officer. I think so. I think he knows what's good for him. But she . . . I wouldn't trust her. I bet she's always been a trouble-maker. You can always tell. This place is a hotbed of agitators.

Soldier (*incredulously*) You don't really fall for that sort of stuff, do you?

Officer. What do you mean?

Soldier (*sceptically*) We-ell. You mean, because they hate Herod, somebody must be puttin' them up to it? When he goes and does things like this? If you ask me, he's not right in the head. If he was in any job except the one he's got, he'd have been locked up years ago.

Officer. It's easy to talk like that, but somebody's got to govern these people. Why do you think the Romans haven't taken the country over? Because they know it's more trouble than it's worth —they'd rather leave Herod here to do it for them. There's always been trouble here, and if you ask me, there always will be. They're a hell of a queer people.

(Rachel *enters, carrying a bowl of water, a cloth and some ointment. She quietly puts them down and listens, unnoticed by the others*)

Soldier (*watching the Officer; quietly, with a frown*) You don't like them, do you?

Officer (*shrugging*) I suppose some of them are all right. But you can't get to grips with them, somehow. They won't fight you back properly, and yet they never really give *in*. You can never really feel you've got them beaten. No. Herod knows the only way to deal with them. Force is the only argument they understand.

Soldier (*looking away; ironically*) Well—at that rate, we argued loud and clear this mornin', didn't we? It ought to be a long time before they forget that little sermon.

Officer (*reacting against the irony in the Soldier's voice*) You talk about a—a minor incident like this as if it was a massacre. A little dead-end hole like Bethlehem—how many babies were there in it altogether? Can't have been more than sixty or seventy. When Herod's dead, do you think anybody's going to remember a little thing like this? He's the one who put Judea on the map. He rebuilt Samaria from almost nothing. Hundreds of years from now, people will still be coming to see the temples in Caesaria. And they'll be saying, "Yes, Herod the Great—that was a man who really understood the meaning of beauty." (*He sinks back with his breathing fatigued, and closes his eyes*)

(*The* Soldier, *out of touch with this kind of talk and rolling his eyes to express his opinion of it, turns, sees Rachel and goes to her*)

Rachel. How is he?
Soldier. Drunk, I'd say. Drunker than me, by some of the rubbish he's been talking.
Rachel. It wasn't even so much his death, I wanted. I wanted to make him suffer in his mind, the way he's made me suffer. I wanted to see him afraid, and pleading, the way my people pleaded with him and got no mercy. I wanted to see him ashamed and disgusted and sick at the thing he's done. But he can't see what he's done. He's blind and deaf with his own pretending. (*She crosses to the Officer and looks down at him*) How can he look so calm as he does? (*She drops down behind him*) How can you talk about these things with the blood of innocent children hardly dry in the streets? (*She rises, gets the body from the manger and shows it to the Officer*) Look!

(*The* Officer *looks at Rachel, unflinching, but not at the child*)

Look! (*She puts the body on the Officer's knees. Loudly*) Look!

(*The* Officer *turns his head aside*)

(*She takes the Officer's head between her hands and turns it forcibly towards the body, pressing down on the back of his head as though she could make him eat it*) Look!

(*The* Officer *closes his eyes*)

(*She comes round to the front of him. With passion*) Is it just being hired by Herod that makes you like that? Or are there men like you in every army? Have they all had their pity torn out by the roots? Are they all such amputated men?

(Rachel *waits so long for the answer that the* Officer *feels impelled to say something*)

Officer. There's nothing to be gained by talking about it.
Rachel. Why don't you want to talk about it? Don't say it makes you uneasy, a man like you, so sure and so right? Why? Have you never heard that kind of talk before?

OFFICER. I've seen that expression in the eyes before; and not so long ago, either.

RACHEL. In whose eyes?

OFFICER. Herod's.

(RACHEL *shuts her eyes tightly and covers them with her fists. There is the sound of footsteps outside. They all listen. RACHEL snatches up the body and puts it in the manger. The SOLDIER goes to the door and looks out into the darkness*)

RACHEL (*moving to the Soldier*) Who was it?

SOLDIER. Nobody. Just a man and a woman going home.

RACHEL. I thought it was Simon.

(*The SOLDIER closes the door*)

SOLDIER (*in confidence*) What's he really gone for? (*He points to the Officer*) He thinks he's gone to fetch the lieutenant. He won't really do that, will he?

RACHEL (*bitterly*) Oh, yes. He'll do it.

SOLDIER. Why? Wasn't it his kid, too?

RACHEL (*nodding*) But Simon—doesn't like trouble. He likes to keep in with—the right people.

SOLDIER (*restively*) Well, look—I—if he's really fetching him, I—I'll have to go, then.

RACHEL. Why?

SOLDIER (*smiling crookedly*) I'm not ready for Elysium, yet, lady.

RACHEL. But he can tell them you came back.

SOLDIER. That won't make no difference.

RACHEL. You mean he'd let them kill you? After you came back to help him?

SOLDIER. They all saw me, see, lady. I went a bit wild and it was in front of the others. He'd have to make an example.

(RACHEL *cannot understand*)

Well, I mean, he'd *have* to, wouldn't he? They wouldn't have no respect for him. (*He crosses to the Officer, bends over him and takes his purse from him*)

(RACHEL *picks up the knife and hides it behind her back*)

I'll have to take this, sir. I'm sorry. But I wouldn't get far without money, would I?

OFFICER. Are you leaving me here wi*h her?

SOLDIER. Got no option, sir. (*He moves to Rachel*) But—(*he takes Rachel by the chin and looks into her eyes*) she'll be all right now. She won't do nothin' now.

OFFICER. What makes you think that?

Soldier. Well—I know women, sir—I even married one of them. They flare up quick, they don't quite know what they're doin' for a bit—but they can't keep it up for long. No proper women; not this kind. (*To Rachel*) Can you?

(Rachel *drops her eyes*)

No, she's better now. (*To Rachel*) Listen. Look after him till they get here, won't you?

Rachel. Everybody tells me that.

Soldier (*gently*) Because they know you're a good girl; and what's done is done; and maybe your husband is right. Neither you nor me can change the world, my pretty—but that's a man down there, whatever he's done. And he's having a lot of pain. And no-one but you can help him because he's as helpless as a newborn . . .

(Rachel's *eyes flash up again, daring him to finish the phrase*)

(*More gently still*) Yes, I know. But you can have more babies. That's if you don't do anythin' stupid and get into worse trouble.

(Rachel's *eyes avoid his again*)

(*He turns her half-round, looks behind her and sees the knife in her hand*) Come on. Come on. Anyway—you can't do it, can you? You tried, and you know you can't do it. (*He holds out his hand*)

(Rachel *slowly brings her hand round and hands him the knife*)

That's better. Now, come here. (*He leads Rachel up* LC, *throws back a wink at the Officer to say it is* "O.K.", *and takes Rachel out of sight of the Officer*) Hold your hand out.

(Rachel *holds out her hand*)

(*He takes some coins from the purse and counts them into Rachel's hand*) This is for looking after him. For his food, I mean, and for the oil, and wine, and whatever you had to get. (*He checks himself, looks into the purse and draws back the last coin he was giving her*) No. I'd better keep the rest for now.

(Rachel *looks with revulsion at the money*)

What's the matter? Not enough? Well, look, if I'm ever in Judea again—after it's all blown over—if you find it comes to more than that, I'll square up with you then. All right? (*He opens the door and looks out*)

Rachel. Good-bye.

(*The* Soldier *puts Rachel's hand over the open palm where the money lies, clasps them both warmly for an instant, then quickly exits.* Rachel *uncovers the money and looks at it, then, holding her hand a little away from her, tilts her palm slowly sideways until the coins slide off one by one and fall with soft thuds to the earthen floor of the stable. She plucks a wisp of hay and wipes her palm with it as if to get rid of some uncleanness. She closes the door. The* OFFICER *looks enquiringly at* RACHEL *who neither speaks nor moves)*

OFFICER. What are you going to do?

RACHEL *(exhausted)* Nothing. He was right. I could never bring myself to kill you. I couldn't bring myself to touch you. I shall do nothing. Except perhaps pray.

OFFICER. To whom?

RACHEL. There is only one God.

OFFICER *(with a slight apologetic smile)* I forgot.

RACHEL. I shall pray that all the soldiers have gone. That Simon searches all night and never finds them. Then I needn't lift a finger. I can just stay here and watch you die.

OFFICER. That would make you happy?

RACHEL *(moving to the manger)* Nothing will make me happy. But it will give me satisfaction. Why don't you pray to Caesar, since you think such a lot of Rome? Don't you believe he can save you?

OFFICER *(dryly)* I think that would hardly be fair on Caesar. The odds against are a bit too heavy. You must remember poor Octavius hasn't been a God very long. *(He coughs)* I'll have to think up something easier for him. A drink of wine, perhaps.

RACHEL. Well? *(She points to the flagon on the shelf* L*)* There it is. Go on, ask Caesar. Or one of your Gaulish gods. They might bring it to you.

(The OFFICER *twists himself over on to his side and painfully inches his way along the bench to the extreme left end, from where he hopes to be able to stretch out his arm and reach the flagon. His breathing is difficult and audible. Once he stops and collapses, as if giving in. He turns a look of entreaty on Rachel, as if hoping even now that she will relent and come to his aid.* RACHEL'S *face is stony and she looks away. The* OFFICER *reaches the end of the bench, where he tries to hoist himself on to the pile of sacks which Simon put there to provide a back-rest for him. He leans far out over them to try to reach the flagon. He has had no opportunity to notice that the bench was designed to hold its heaviest weights in the centre, and that the two perpendicular cross-pieces supporting it are not placed at the ends but some way in from each end, so that the sacks are lying beyond the left-hand "leg" of the bench, although up to now the dead weight of the Officer in the centre has counter-balanced them and kept the bench stable. As the* OFFICER *reaches out, his weight added to the weight of the grain is too much. As his fingers almost close on the flagon the bench suddenly upsets. The sacks slide to the ground, and with*

a loud cry of pain the Officer *falls to the ground in a twisted heap.*
Rachel *is horrified. She backs away to the manger*)

No! No! I don't want to see. (*She closes her eyes and turns her head
aside*) Oh, God, oh, Jehovah, let him die quickly and get it over
with. Oh, God, Jehovah, tell me what to do. If he hadn't been so
stubborn, if he would only have seen his wickedness and been
ashamed, he could have lived. I would have let him live.

(*The* Officer *coughs*)

No! (*She turns and clings to the manger and presses her face against it*)
You're asking too much. Oh, God, it's too much to ask of anybody.

Officer (*with great difficulty; in a loud, harsh, unrelenting voice*)   I
haven't asked you—for anything.

Rachel (*distracted*) Somebody is. I'm sure I heard somebody. I
think I'm going out of my mind. Nobody would ask such a mon-
strous thing. (*She stretches out a hand to David's body*) David, was it
you, my darling? Darling, I can't! You don't understand. This is
the man who came to kill you. There are some things it would be
wicked to forgive. (*With all her strength, as if answering a voice in her
own mind, and trying to drown it*) He knew, he knew what he was
doing! (*She looks round at the Officer*)

(*The* Officer's *state is pitiful*)

(*She is almost drawn to him, almost goes. She turns away and holds tight
to the manger as if to make herself proof against temptation*) Hold me,
hold me! (*She writhes*) I don't understand what is happening.
(*Wildly*) My labour is over, I had a son; there's no more to come
out of me now. (*She turns her head to address the Officer. Defiantly*)
There's nothing left, I tell you. Don't you hear me? You think
because I am a woman there's gentleness in me, and pity—but they
were my son's and no-one shall have them now. (*She loosens her grip
on the manger to put her hand to her head and shield her eyes from the light*)
It's only my head that's bursting—it's the light. (*She moves towards
the Officer, her voice still scolding, but her movements are almost a sleep-
walker's, as if directed by a force outside her control*) You think because
you lie there dumb and helpless—(*a sort of sobbing breaks through
the accusation in her tone*) that I'd be stupid enough to . . . (*She pulls
the bench and one of the sacks aside and looks at the Officer with horror and
guilt and the beginning of pity*)

(*The* Officer *coughs*)

(*She winces*) Will you please not do that? (*She bends over him*) I know
quite well why you do it. You think, just because I've borne a
man and seen what a pitiful thing he is . . . (*She closes her eyes*) No,

it's too much, it's too much! (*She examines the wound*) Oh, God, oh, Jehovah! (*She covers her face with her hands and weeps, and drops on her knees beside him, beaten. When she lifts her head, her face and voice are washed clean of all passion: she is quiet and sane and kind. Sorrowfully and gently*) Soldier.

(*For the first time the* OFFICER *and* RACHEL *look at each other without murder between them, with shame on both sides and hostility on neither*)

(*Softly*) Oh, what did they do to you, what did they ever do to make you so blind? What did they do to you, soldier, that you couldn't see what you were doing to us?

(*The* OFFICER *is silent*)

All right. Now just—lie quiet. (*Her voice is now the one she must have used for David*) There. That's the way. Don't be afraid. Nobody's going to hurt you. (*She rises, goes to the bowl of water and soaks the cloth in it. She is peaceful, emptied and mildly wondering*) Do you know where this came from? (*She wrings out the cloth*) That woman had her baby wrapped in it, until Martha gave her a better piece. I'm glad that one lived. Poor little mite—He was so light and quiet in my arms. (*She takes the cover from her ointment and places it by the folded cloth, then tears a strip from her own head-scarf to serve as bandage*) If He'd know what you were trying to do to Him, I wonder if He'd been willing to leave anything behind to bind your wounds. (*She goes to the Officer, kneels beside him and bandages the wound*) All right, all right. It isn't going to hurt, not much. Sh! Sh! There.

(SIMON *enters, stamps his boots and unwinds his scarf*)

SIMON (*puffing*) What a night! *I* don't know what to do. Searched the town, no *sign* of a lieutenant. Some of them think he's gone back to Jerusalem to make a report. Couldn't even find a soldier for a long time. Ask me, they've all gone a bit jittery. They don't quite know what's happened. (*He closes the door. His voice and movements are noisy*)

RACHEL (*frowning*) Sh!

SIMON (*crossing to Rachel; quietly*) What's the matter? How is he?

RACHEL. He's unconscious. But I think he's going to be all right. Fetch me a blanket.

SIMON (*looking down at the Officer*) Oh, yes. You're doing a good job there, Rachel. I told him that. "If I tell her to do it," I said, "she'll do it."

RACHEL (*with patient irony*) Yes, Simon. (*She is preoccupied and concerned over the Officer*) Fetch me a blanket, will you?

SIMON. All right. (*He hunts vaguely around*) Lucky for him it happened here. "You'd find no better nurse anywhere", I told him, "than Rachel." I can't find any blanket.

(*The first light of dawn appears through the window*)

RACHEL. In the back stall.

SIMON (*going into the back stall*) It's getting light. (*He gives an exclamation of pleased discovery*) Rachel! Come and look.

RACHEL. The blanket, Simon.

(SIMON *brings a blanket from the stall and hands it to Rachel*)

(*She covers the Officer. With grave tenderness*) Yes. He'll be all right. (*Only then, for the first time, does she take her eyes off the Officer to attend to Simon*) Look at what? (*She rises*)

SIMON (*moving to the back stall*) That lamb the boy left here— remember? I thought it was as good as dead, didn't you? Well, come here—just look at him. (*He puts an arm around Rachel's shoulder and draws her to the door of the stall*)

RACHEL (*almost smiling*) He's trying to stand up.

SIMON. I'd never have believed there was that much life in it. I wonder—I wonder if it's going to live?

As they watch the lamb's efforts with absorption, the daylight lightens outside the window. A few birds begin the dawn chorus and their song is swelled by a tentative bleat. SIMON and RACHEL look at one another and then back into the stall as—

the CURTAIN *falls*

FURNITURE AND PROPERTY LIST

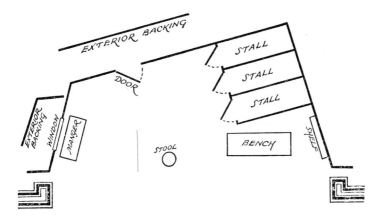

SCENE I

On stage: Bench. *On it:* bucket, open sack of grain, Rachel's headscarf
Sacks of grain
Shelf (down L) *On it:* wine jars, jar of water, beaker, lamp
Milking stool
Manger, with three new slats. *In it:* hay
Pile of hay (down R)
Wooden and earthenware implements
On hook L: old cloak
In stall up L: milk
Down L: light wooden rake
In back stall: blanket

Personal: RACHEL: 2 gold coins, pot of frankincense

SCENE II

Set: Bucket from bench to floor
      Spilled sack of corn on left end of bench
        On floor LC: bloodstained knife

Off stage: Flagon of wine, beaker (RACHEL)
           Bottle of wine (SOLDIER)
           Food (SOLDIER)
           Baby (RACHEL)
           Bowl of water, cloth, ointment (RACHEL)

Personal: OFFICER: belt, knife and sheath, purse with coins
          SOLDIER: coin

LIGHTING PLOT

Property fittings required: oil lamp
    Interior. A stable. The same scene throughout
    THE MAIN ACTING AREAS are C, R and down L
    THE APPARENT SOURCES OF LIGHT are a window R and a door up R,
    and at night, an oil lamp R

SCENE I. Early morning

To open: Effect of early morning daylight

Cue 1   At end of Scene   (Page 9)
        · *Dim to* BLACK-OUT

SCENE II. Late afternoon

To open: Effect of sunset

Cue 2   After rise of CURTAIN   (Page 10)
        Slow cross fade of lights from sunset to twilight effect

Cue 3   The SOLDIER lights the lamp   (Page 28)
        Bring up covering light R on manger

Cue 4   SIMON: ". . . find any blanket."   (Page 37)
        Bring up lights for dawn effect

EFFECTS PLOT

SCENE I

Cue 1   At rise of CURTAIN   (Page 1)

Rural morning noises, crowing and lowing and the rattle and splash of a well-bucket

Cue 2   SIMON: "... what to say."   (Page 7)

Sound of a baby whining
Sound of distant drums

Cue 3   SIMON: "No, not that."   (Page 7)

The sound of the drums grows louder

Cue 4   SIMON: "... door a minute."   (Page 7)

The sound of the drums grows louder
A lamb bleats
The sound of the drums reaches a peak then starts to fade

Cue 5   RACHEL: "... the market-place."   (Page 8)

The drums cease

SCENE II

Cue 6   SIMON: "... going to live."   (Page 37)

Sound of birds' dawn chorus and a lamb's bleat